Telepathy, Genuine And Fraudulent

- William Wortley Baggally -

PART I

GENUINE TELEPATHY

Sir William F. Barrett, one of the founders of the Society for Psychical Research, more than forty years ago tried some experiments which led him to believe that something then new to science, which he provisionally called "thought transference" and which is now known as "telepathy," really existed.

At the first general meeting of the Society, on the 17th July 1882, he read a paper entitled "First Report on Mind Reading."

Since that date the Society has carried out a great number of experiments which tend to show that telepathy is a scientific fact. The evidence for its existence is twofold—that which can be gathered experimentally, and that which arises spontaneously. To the first category belong those experiments in the transmission of the images of drawings or diagrams by means of an effort of the will of a person known as the *agent* to the mind of another person designated the *percipient*, when the transmission is carried out otherwise than through the ordinary channel of the senses. To the second category belong those hallucinations of seeing a person at the moment of death or at a crisis, evidence for which has been obtained abundantly by the Society for Psychical Research and has been embodied in the work *Phantasms of the Living*, and in the *Census of Hallucinations*—a report on which appeared in the *Proceedings* of the Society in 1894.

There are several theories to explain the action of telepathy. The first compares it to wireless telegraphy. On this hypothesis it is supposed that it is due to ethereal wave action:—Thought causes motion in the brain cells of the agent, the cells then impart motion to the surrounding ether in the form of waves which impinge on the brain cells of the percipient and give rise to a corresponding thought to that which started the ethereal wave motion.

This theory offers great difficulties. An opponent to it points out that "A wireless message is transmitted by a succession of single ethereal wave impulses produced by the electric sparks at the starting station and received by the coherer at the receiving station, whereas a diagram to be transmitted would require a number of brain-waves produced simultaneously and arranged in the form of the diagram."

Another mode of putting the matter recently advanced is that the agent does not transmit his thought, but that the percipient reads clairvoyantly what is in the agent's mind.

There is also the spiritualistic theory. It is asserted that an external entity, or spirit, conveys the images or thoughts from one mind to another.

Another theory is that telepathy takes place in the subconscious mind, and that the subconscious mind of the agent is in communication with the subconscious mind of the percipient by means of the universal mind underlying all things and of which individual subconscious minds form part.

Not one of these theories has been accepted as proved by the Society for Psychical Research. In cases of spontaneous telepathy it is now generally believed that the appearance of a person at the time of death or at a crisis is not caused by an objective bodily ghost, but arises from a telepathic impact from the agent formulating itself into his image in the mind of the percipient.

In the case of two persons seeing an apparition at the same time, this may be due to the two percipients receiving each, separately, a telepathic impression, or there may be only one percipient who telepathically impresses the hallucination on the mind of the second person.

I will now proceed to relate some cases of telepathy which have come under my personal observation. My first experiment in the transmission of images of drawings and diagrams took place in the rooms of the Society for Psychical Research in May 1902. A private lady, Miss M. Telbin, acted as percipient, and I acted as agent. There were present at the time Mr. J. G. Piddington, Honorary Secretary of the Society, and Mr. Thomas, the then Acting Secretary.

During the first experiment Miss Telbin, who was a stranger to me, sat with her back towards a large opaque screen. In front of her stood a small table upon which rested a crystal ball. She was asked to gaze at the crystal and to describe any vision that might appear to form itself therein. I may parenthetically remark that the object of crystal-gazing is to concentrate the mind and to withdraw it from outward influences. The vision seen in the crystal does not exist objectively, but only in the mind of the seer. On the other side of the screen, entirely hidden from the view of Miss Telbin, sat Mr. Piddington and myself. This gentleman proceeded to take from a box, which was behind the screen and on the floor between his and my chairs, various articles, and to hand them silently, one at a time, to me. I then concentrated my thoughts successively on each article. Miss Telbin gave an account of what she saw in the crystal, and Mr. Thomas, who sat in such a position that both Mr. Piddington and myself were hidden from his view, took notes of what occurred.

The first article handed me was a *Windsor Magazine*, on the cover of which there was an engraving of Windsor Castle. I concentrated my thoughts on this engraving, and Miss Telbin then gave a description of the vision that presented itself to her mental view.

She first observed that she could see trees on the left side of the picture, and cottages also on the left, and that there was water.

These details were correct so far as they went, but the subsequent details that she gave were incorrect, and the experiment was abandoned as a failure. I then replaced the magazine in the box from which it had been taken, so that Miss Telbin had no opportunity of seeing the magazine during the experiment nor after.

Other experiments were being tried when Miss Telbin spontaneously said that she had had a vision of Windsor Castle.

This experiment may be regarded as a case of deferred telepathy.

Another experiment with the same lady, in which simultaneous double telepathy occurred, is of better evidential value.

Miss Telbin again sat with her back to the screen, and instead of the crystal a piece of paper and a pencil were placed on the table in front of her.

This time Mr. Thomas and I sat behind the screen hidden from her view, and Mr. J. G. Piddington took notes. Mr. Thomas and I acted as simultaneous agents. We each held a small piece of cardboard with a diagram on it known to the agent viewing it, but not to the other agent. These diagrams belonged to the Society for Psychical Research and had not been seen by Mr. Thomas nor by me previous to the experiment. They were in a box which was at our feet behind the screen. We each took a diagram from the box, taking care that we did not see each other's diagram.

We concentrated our minds on our respective diagrams, and Miss Telbin drew her impressions on the piece of paper in front of her. The following drawings show the results:—

MR. BAGGALLY'S
DIAGRAM.

MISS TELBIN'
DRAWING.

MR. THOMAS'S
DIAGRAM.

MISS TELBIN'S
DRAWING.

At the time that Miss Telbin got the impression of the diagram with three sections, she made the remark that it looked like three leaves.

The correspondence between the drawings and the diagrams is very great, and difficult to account for by chance.

The following points have to be considered. First, that Miss Telbin only made two drawings and not many from which two might have been selected in which there was a resemblance to the diagrams. Secondly, that Mr.

Thomas's diagram was correctly reproduced although in a reversed position (the reversal of a figure sometimes happens in experiments in telepathy). Thirdly, that my diagram of three triangles, although not reproduced in the form of triangles, was drawn correctly as regards there being three sections, and that the relative position of the sections was given correctly. Fourthly, that Miss Telbin had not previously seen any of the diagrams, and therefore the chances against her being able to hit upon any diagram which was then being used were very great. Fifthly, that the chances against her being able to hit upon two diagrams simultaneously were even greater.

The explanation that the result might have been due to collusion between the persons experimenting of course cannot be entertained, at least by myself, who was one of the experimenters.

It was not possible for the percipient to see through the large screen which was behind her, and there were no mirrors in the room in which the small diagrams could have been reflected. No word was spoken to give her the slightest clue. These two successful telepathic experiments led to further ones at a distance between this lady and myself.

It will be of interest to insert here an account of an experiment in telepathy, similar to the one I have just described, between two agents and one percipient, which Sir Oliver Lodge carried out in the year 1884.

When the experiment was tried with Miss Telbin, Mr. Thomas, and myself I was not aware that Sir Oliver Lodge had already tried an experiment of a like nature.

Sir Oliver Lodge's Account

"My own first actual experience of thought transference, or experimental telepathy, was obtained in the years 1883 and 1884 at Liverpool, when I was invited by Mr. Malcolm Guthrie of that city to join in an investigation which he was conducting with the aid of one or two persons who had turned out to be sensitive, from among the employees of the large drapery firm of George Henry Lee & Co.

"A large number of these experiments had been conducted before I was asked to join, throughout the spring and autumn of 1883, but it is better for me to adhere strictly to my own experience and to relate only those experiments over which I had control.

"Most of these experiments were confirmations of the kind of thing that had been observed by other experimenters. But one experiment which I tried was definitely novel, and, as it seems to me, important; since it clearly showed that when two agents are acting, each contributes to the effect, and that the result is due, not to one alone, but to both combined. The experiment is thus described by me in the columns of *Nature*, vol. xxx., page 145, for 12th June 1884:—

"An Experiment in Thought Transference

"Those of your readers who are interested in the subject of thought transference, now being investigated, may be glad to hear of a little experiment which I recently tried here. The series of experiments was originated and carried on in this city by Mr. Malcolm Guthrie, and he has prevailed on me, on Dr. Herdman, and on one or two other more or less scientific witnesses, to be present on several occasions, critically to examine the conditions, and to impose any fresh ones that we thought desirable. I need not enter into particulars, but I will just say that the conditions under which apparent transference of thought occurs from one or more persons, steadfastly thinking, to another in the same room blindfold and wholly disconnected from the others, seem to me absolutely satisfactory, and such as to preclude the possibility of conscious collusion on the one hand or unconscious muscular indication on the other.

"One evening last week—after two thinkers, or agents, had been several times successful in instilling the idea of some object or drawing, at which they were looking, into the mind of the blindfold person, or percipient—I brought into the room a double opaque sheet of thick paper with a square drawn on one side and a St. Andrew's cross or X on the other, and silently arranged it between the two agents so that each looked on one side without any notion of what was on the other. The percipient was not informed in any way that a novel modification was being made; and, as usual, there was no contact of any sort or kind—a clear space of several feet existing between each of the three people. I thought that by this variation I should decide whether one of the two agents was more active than the other; or, supposing them about equal, whether two ideas in two separate minds could be fused into one by the percipient.

"In a very short time the percipient made the following remarks, every one else being silent: 'The thing won't keep still.' 'I seem to see things moving about.' 'First I see a thing up there, and then one down there.' 'I can't see either distinctly.' The object was then hidden, and the percipient was told to take off the bandage and to draw the impression in her mind on a sheet of paper. She drew a square, and then said, 'There was the other thing as well,' and drew a cross inside the square from corner to corner, saying afterwards, 'I don't know what made me put it inside.'

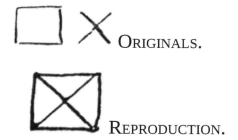

ORIGINALS.

REPRODUCTION.

"The experiment is no more conclusive as evidence than fifty others that I have seen at Mr. Guthrie's, but it seems to me somewhat interesting that two minds should produce a disconnected sort of impression on the mind of the percipient, quite different from the single impression which we had usually obtained when two agents were both looking at the same thing. Once, for instance (to take a nearly corresponding case under those conditions), when the object was a rude drawing of the main lines in a Union Jack, the figure was reproduced by the percipient as a whole without misgiving; except, indeed, that she expressed a doubt as to whether its middle horizontal line were present or not, and ultimately omitted it."

ORIGINAL.

 REPRODUCTION.

As I have said, the two successful telepathic experiments which I have described, and which took place in the rooms of the Society for Psychical Research, led to further experiments at a distance between Miss Telbin and myself.

AT 7 P.M.	AT 7 P.M.
I drew the following diagram	Miss TELBIN's drawings
AT 7:10 P.M.	AT 7:10 P.M.
I fixed my attention on a flower	Miss TELBIN obtained several incorrect scrawls, but amongst them one under which she had written the words "First impression"
AT 7:20 P.M.	AT 7:20 P.M.
I looked at a pair of opera glasses, at which I gazed first lengthwise	Miss TELBIN's drawings were—

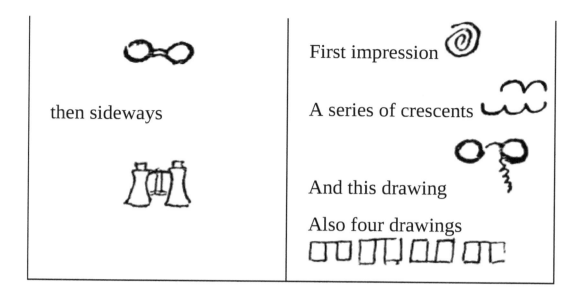

then sideways

First impression

A series of crescents

And this drawing

Also four drawings

It was arranged that we should sit on certain days in the week, and that at a fixed hour I should act as agent and transmit to her my thoughts, she being at the time in her residence in West Hampstead, and I in Kensington. The distance between these localities as the crow flies is four miles. The result of our first sitting, which took place on 20th May 1902, is shown on the preceding page.

There was no possibility that the agent or the percipient could have copied the drawings, as the letters embodying them that we wrote to each other were posted on the evening of the same day and received by the first post the following morning, having crossed in the post.

Telepathy was clearly indicated in this experiment.

We continued trying experiments for some months after, but did not get such good results as at the beginning. On one occasion, however, we obtained a successful negative result. I was not feeling well, and did not fix my attention on any object. On the following morning Miss Telbin's letter said, "I could get nothing from you last night." It was, to say the least, curious that she should not have received an impression on the only night that I had not attempted to experiment.

On another occasion, when Miss Telbin was in London and I in Folkestone, I arranged to transmit to her the impression of a diagram on a certain day at 8 p.m. It chanced that on that evening there was a performance at the theatre, at which my wife wished to be present. I therefore decided to telegraph to Miss Telbin that I would be unable to try the experiment that night, but after a good deal of hesitation I changed my mind, and thought that I would endeavour to transmit the impression of the diagram on my way to the theatre. The letter that I received from Miss Telbin the next day was to this effect:—

"I got a good deal of writing last night which was illegible, but amongst it I read the words 'going out' and 'rain.'"

Now this may be a mere coincidence, but it was strange that the words "going out" should correctly represent the idea that was in my mind during a great part of the preceding day. I had much worried, hesitating whether I should telegraph or not.

The result appears to indicate the transmission of my mental state. The word "rain" represented correctly the state of the weather at Folkestone, but, as it often rains in England, this was of no evidential value.

In regard to spontaneous telepathy I may bring before the reader two cases which I personally investigated, the percipient in the first case being a gentleman who belonged to a circle which regularly met for the study of psychic phenomena, and of which circle I was a member.

The percipient, Mr. John Polley, gave me an account of his vision as follows:—

"At a séance held within sound of Big Ben on 8th May 1901, there were present Mrs. E. V. M., Mr. Thomas Atwood, and myself. As Mr. Atwood resumed his seat after delivering an address (about 8.30 p.m.) I became aware of a vision which presented itself as being some five feet distant from me, and displayed part of the interior of a room, namely, that part where the stove stood. The fire in the stove was small and dull, and close beside it was an overturned chair. In front of the fire was something that looked like a fire-guard or clothes-horse, but this was not clear to me. Playing, or climbing over this article, was a child, who fell forward, and when it regained its feet I noticed that its dress was on fire. I made no reference to the matter at the time, as I had an impression that the vision might be connected with some occurrence in the family of Mrs. M., and I was averse to mentioning it for fear of awakening sad memories. Shortly afterwards the whole vision was repeated, and this time I had an uncontrollable impulse to speak. Upon describing what I had seen for the second time, I was much relieved to hear that the matter was not recognized as being connected in any way with the sitters. I may mention here that the child appeared to be about three years old, and, judging from the style of dress, I described it as a girl, although the vision would apply equally to a boy, as at that early age the short clothes worn by both sexes would be very similar.

"Next Thursday morning, 9th May 1901, upon awakening, I described to my wife the events of the previous evening's séance. On the evening of the same day, namely, Thursday, 9th May, I was out with a friend, and upon my return home at 11.50 p.m., my sister, Mary Louisa Polley, who resided with me at the time, made the remark, 'I have a piece of bad news for you.' 'Well,' I replied, 'what is it? Let me know.' And she answered, 'Brother George's little son, Jacky, has been burned to death.' Like a flash I realized the connexion of the sad event with my vision of the previous night. I then asked my sister, 'How did you know this, and when?' She replied, 'Mr. Fred Sinnett told me when he came over to see us this evening.'

(Signed) "JOHN POLLEY"

I obtained from the other sitters at the séance the following statement:—

"At the séance held on the evening of Wednesday, 8th May 1901, at which were present Mrs. E. V. M., Mr. Thomas Atwood, and Mr. John Polley, we, the undersigned, testify that Mr. John Polley gave to us a description of a vision of the burning of a child which he saw at this séance.

(Signed in full)   "E. V. M.
                    "THOMAS ATWOOD"

I personally interviewed Mr. John Polley's wife and sister and received a written statement from each confirming Mr. Polley's account.

A local paper containing an account of the inquest on the child states that the accident took place on Tuesday, 7th May, and the child was taken to a hospital immediately and there died. The father of the child wrote to me as follows:—

"DEAR SIR,—In reply to your inquiry respecting my late son, John Frederick, I beg to say that on Tuesday, 7th May, my wife went out to do some shopping, leaving my son, aged two years and two months, in a bedroom with another brother aged seven. Whilst the elder brother was getting some toys to play with, the deceased thrust some paper in the fire, pulled it out again, and set fire to his clothes. Some neighbours took him to the Children's Hospital, Paddington Green, where he passed away on Wednesday, 8th May, at 11.45 a.m. No intimation of this was given by myself or any member of our family to my brother, Mr. John Polley, until a friend of the family called at my address on Thursday, 9th May, between 1 and 2 p.m., when we informed him of the sad loss that we had sustained, and he told us that he intended calling on my brother that evening, and we asked him if he would communicate the news to my brother and sister who reside at Church Street, Stoke Newington. Of course, Sir, you know I am antagonistic to your views, but my brother has told me it is for the interests of science. If this is so, I take great pleasure in its furtherance.—Yours sincerely,

(Signed) "FREDERICK GEORGE POLLEY"

In the above case it appears to me that the vision of the burning child which Mr. John Polley saw arose out of a spontaneous telepathic impression, either from the mind of the father of the child to his brother's (Mr. John Polley's mind), or from the mind of one of the persons who was cognizant of the sad event.

In regard to the second case of spontaneous telepathy to which I have referred, I cannot do better than to give the account of same as it appeared in the *Journal of the Society for Psychical Research* of June 1912:—

"The following case of a reciprocal telepathic impression occurring to two persons at the same time has been communicated to us by Mr. W. W. Baggally. Both Miss Emma Steele and Mr. Claude Burgess, the lady and gentleman concerned in the case, are known personally to Mr. Baggally.

"Miss Steele writes as follows:—

> "'16 and 17 SILLWOOD PLACE,
> "'BRIGHTON, 13*th March* 1912

"'Mr. Claude Burgess, who is an invalid, had been staying at my private hotel, at the above address, for some months. He left on 15th February to take up his residence at No. 10 Belgrave Place, Kemp Town, Brighton. In the interval between the date of his leaving and the night of the 5th inst., when I had the remarkable dream (if it can be called a dream) which I am about to relate, I had not seen Mr. Burgess, and nothing had occurred to cause me to think particularly about him.

"'On the above night I retired to rest at my usual time. I awoke finding myself standing in the middle of my room and answering, "All right, I'm coming," to Mr. Burgess, who, I thought, called three times: "Miss Steele! Miss Steele! Miss Steele!"

"'By the time I had put on my dressing-gown and lighted the gas I was fully awake. I then remembered Mr. Burgess was no longer in the house. I looked at the clock and noticed it was exactly 3 a.m. When I came downstairs next morning I told my cook my dream, and remarked I hoped nothing had happened to Mr. Burgess. During the next day, Wednesday, 6th March, in the afternoon, a man called while I was out and left a note from Mr. Burgess, which I enclose. I was much surprised by its contents. It struck me most forcibly getting it from him, as he is paralysed and has to write with great difficulty with his left hand. He very seldom writes now, so it must have made a great impression on him seeing me as he relates in his letter.

"'EMMA M. STEELE'

"The letter from Mr. Burgess to Miss Steele referred to above, which is now in our possession, was as follows:—

"'10 BELGRAVE PLACE, BRIGHTON

"'MY DEAR EMMA,—I had a funny dream about you last night. I dreamed that you appeared at about 3 a.m. Just a glimpse of you. It's funny, isn't it?—Yours,

"'CLAUDE BURGESS'

"Miss Steele's cook made the following statement to Mr. Baggally:—

"'13th March 1912

"'On Wednesday morning, the 6th March last, Miss Emma Steele came down from her bedroom at 8.30. I saw she was looking pale. I asked her if she were not well. She replied that she had had a strange dream. She heard Mr. Burgess call her three times. She told me that she suddenly jumped up and put her dressing-gown on. By the time she had put on her dressing-gown and lit the gas she remembered Mr. Burgess had left the house. She said it was about 3 o'clock a.m. when she heard Mr. Burgess call.

(Signed)   "'SARAH POLLARD'

"The following statement was written by Mr. Baggally on 13th March 1912, from Mr. Claude Burgess's dictation:—

"'On Tuesday night, 5th March 1912, I woke up at about 3 a.m. with a start. I saw Miss Emma Steele standing at the door of my bedroom. I had closed the door, but she appeared to have opened it. She was attired in her ordinary dress.

"'I was much surprised. It was an absolutely distinct apparition. I had not been thinking of her the previous day, and I cannot tell why she appeared to me.

"'The apparition lasted about five seconds. I was not at all frightened, and went to sleep immediately after.

"'I was so struck by what I had seen that, next morning, the 6th March, at about 11 o'clock, I wrote a letter to Miss Steele which I handed to Mr. William Watkins, the proprietor of the establishment where I now reside, for him to send to Miss Steele. In this letter I told Miss Steele that I had dreamed that she had appeared to me on the previous night.

(Signed)   "'CLAUDE BURGESS'

"In reply to Mr. Baggally's personal inquiries, Mr. Claude Burgess stated that it was the first time that he had had a hallucination of this kind, and he had not had one since.

Statement by Mr. William Watkins

"'10 BELGRAVE PLACE,
"'BRIGHTON, 13*th March* 1912

"'Mr. Claude Burgess delivered to me a letter which he had written to Miss Steele, at about 11 a.m. on 6th March, which I handed to a man of the Church Army Labour Home to take to Miss Steele. The same morning at 8 a.m. Mr. Burgess told me he had dreamt of Miss Steele.

"'WILLIAM WATKINS'

Statement by Mr. Baggally

"'I called on the afternoon of the 13th March 1912 at the offices of the Church Army Labour Home, St. James Street, Brighton, and saw the Secretary, who showed me an entry in their books confirming the fact that, at the request of Mr. William Watkins, a man in their employ had delivered a letter to Miss Emma Steele of 16 Sillwood Place, Brighton, in the afternoon of 6th March 1912.

"'I have interviewed all the persons connected with this case, and they confirmed their respective statements.

"'W. W. Baggally'

"In reply to our further questions as to whether Mr. Burgess's experience was a dream or a waking hallucination, Mr. Baggally wrote to us on 1st April 1912:—

"'I had an interview with Mr. Burgess to-day, and the following is the information I received from him respecting the points you raise. He said to me:—

"""(1) I used the word 'dream' in my letter to Miss Steele for want of a better word. (2) I woke up and then had the vision of Miss Steele. (3) I did not notice anything in the room at the time I had the vision. The room appeared dark. (4) Miss Steele appeared to me in a bright light, not self-luminous or phosphorescent, but just as she would have appeared in daylight. She appeared to me in the part of the room where the door was.'"

"Mrs. Baggally sends us the following statement enclosed in a letter dated 27th April 1912:—

"'I was in the drawing-room of Miss E. Steele's sister on the evening of Wednesday, 6th March, when Miss Emma Steele came in, saying in an excited manner, "Where is Mr. Baggally? He will be so interested in this."

"'She held in her hand a letter from Mr. Burgess, and proceeded to tell me that the previous night she had heard, as she thought, Mr. Burgess fall on the floor of the bedroom over her own. She sprang out of bed.

"'Finding herself in the middle of the room, she heard him call "Miss Steele!" three times. She then suddenly remembered that Mr. Burgess was no longer living in her hotel. She struck a light, looked at the clock, and found it was 3 o'clock. The following morning she felt so tired that when giving orders to her cook, the latter noticed her fatigue and commented upon it. She told the cook the reason was that she heard Mr. Burgess apparently calling her at 3 o'clock.

"'Miss Steele proceeded to say that Mr. Burgess had, curiously enough, sent her that afternoon the note which at that moment she held in her hand, and in which he told her that he dreamt she had appeared to him at 3 a.m. the previous night.

"'Miss Steele appeared much impressed and wondered if anything had happened to Mr. Burgess. I informed my husband that same night, on his return home, of what Miss E. Steele had told me.

"'LAURA E. BAGGALLY'

"'On my return home on the evening of 6th March my wife related to me what appears in her statement above.

"'W. W. BAGGALLY'"

The above case is evidentially a good one, inasmuch as both Miss Emma Steele and Mr. Burgess each reported on the morning of 6th March (the one to her cook and the other to his landlord) their experiences of the previous night before either of them was aware that a reciprocal telepathic impression had occurred between them.

There appears to be evidence that telepathy can also occur between the mind of a human being and that of an animal. The reader will doubtless recollect Mr. H. Rider Haggard's case which appeared in the public press. This gentleman, on the night of Saturday, 9th July 1904, dreamed that a favourite dog of his eldest daughter was lying on its side among brushwood by water, and that it was trying to transmit in an undefined fashion the knowledge that it was dying. Next day the dog was missing. The body of the dog was subsequently found floating in the water near a bridge. An examination of the attendant circumstances pointed to the dog having met its death on the night of Mr. Rider Haggard's dream. As a result of this gentleman having made public this experience, he received from numerous correspondents accounts of telepathy between the minds of the writers of the letters and the minds of animals. These accounts were sent by Mr. Rider Haggard to the Secretary of the S.P.R., who handed them to me for investigation.

A very good case was that communicated by Lady C. The following is the account of her experience:—

"On one hot Sunday afternoon in the summer of 1900 I went, after luncheon, to pay my customary visit to the stables to give sugar and carrots to the horses, among the number being a favourite mare named Kitty. She was a shy, nervous, well-bred animal, and there existed between us a great and unusual sympathy. I used to ride her every morning before breakfast (whatever the weather might be)—quiet, solitary rides on the cliffs which overhung the sea at Castle F., and it always seemed to me that Kitty enjoyed that hour in the freshness of the day as much as I did. On this particular afternoon I left the stables, and walked along to the garden, a distance of a quarter of a mile, and established myself under a tree with an interesting book, fully intending to remain there for a couple of hours. After about twenty minutes an uncomfortable sensation came between me and my reading, and at once I felt sure that there was something the matter with Kitty. I tried to put the feeling from me, and to go on with my book, but the impression grew stronger, and I felt compelled to hasten back to the stables. I went straight to Kitty's box and found her 'cast,' and in urgent need of help. The stablemen were in a distant part of the stables, whence I fetched them to have the mare up. Their surprise was great to find me in the stables for the second time that afternoon."

I wrote to Lady C., and received the following reply:—

"27*th December* 1904

"Lady C. would be glad indeed to have the case investigated, as it always seemed to her to be of the greatest possible interest. At the same time, it may be difficult at this date to get a statement from the stablemen, one of whom is somewhere in England, but Lady C. will try to do so. She is absolutely convinced that no one entered the stable. Had the stablemen done so they would at once have helped the mare to get up, and anyone else would have given the alarm. It seems a direct case of telepathy from animal mind to human."

Lady C. afterwards sent me a statement from a former coachman; it is this:—

"31*st December* 1904

"I was coachman at Castle F. at the time. Lady C. came to the stables after luncheon as usual on a Sunday afternoon with carrots and sugar for the horses. Kitty was then loose in her box and quite well. I then went to my room over the stables, the other stablemen being also upstairs, and to my surprise, after half an hour or three-quarters of an hour later, her ladyship, who had been to the garden, called me and the other stablemen to come and help Kitty up, as she was lying 'cast'[1] in her box. No one had gone into the stable in the interval.

(Signed)   "E. N."

Telepathy may possibly exist between the mind of an animal and that of a human being and *vice versa*, but a sufficient number of cases have not been collected to establish this as a fact.

PART II

FRAUDULENT TELEPATHY

I now come to another class of so-called thought transference—that exhibited at public entertainments in which genuine telepathy plays no part.

On the 25th November 1912 Miss Isabel Newton, the Secretary of the Society for Psychical Research, and I attended the demonstration given by Yoga [*sic*] Rama of his alleged occult powers at the "Little Theatre," Adelphi.

Accounts had appeared in the public press of a previous private performance given by this so-called Abyssinian Mystic, at which Sir John Simon, the Solicitor-General, Mr. Bernard Shaw, and Mr. Anthony Hope had assisted, and it was stated that Yoga Rama had been able to read the thoughts of the Solicitor-General by supernormal means.

In order to demonstrate, in a public manner, the alleged occult power of this "psychic," a stage performance was given at the "Little Theatre" on the afternoon of the above-mentioned date. A large audience was present, and their expectations of witnessing manifestations of an occult nature were raised by the contents of the programme, wherein it appeared that Yoga Rama was to give a demonstration of "The power of mind over mind" by means of—

"1. Clairaudience.

"2. The possibility of the interpretation of vibrations without the aid of sound.

"3. Psychometry by sense of touch.

"4. Telepathy. The disclosure of names thought of by persons in the audience.

"5. Disclosure of personalities by subconscious means.

"6. Revelations by a circumstantial chain of mind pictures.

"7. Various demonstrations of ideas silently conveyed to the spectator by suggestion.

"8. Descriptions of cities and places by mind pictures.

"9. Messages."

Before Yoga Rama made his appearance a gentleman (a Mr. Fletcher) delivered a short speech from the stage. He stated that the "Yoga" had acquired his occult powers by contemplation after many years' study. He went on to say that in the Eastern World the occult powers of the mind had been more studied than in the Western World, but at the present day the Western World looked upon these powers with much less prejudice than formerly.

After Mr. Fletcher had retired, Yoga Rama made his appearance from between the centre of two curtains which hung at the back of the stage. He was attired in a long loose black gown and wore a large crimson turban. He advanced to the front of the stage and made a speech which had a smattering of a theosophical discourse. He described four kinds of Yogi. The first kind, he said, was frequently met in India. These Yogi worked on the physical plane and produced effects resembling the feats of a conjurer. The second kind worked in the mental plane (to this class he implied that he belonged). The third dealt with the spiritual problems of life. The fourth was absorbed in meditation.

He continued his speech by saying that he required the sympathy of the persons with whom he would experiment. If they mentally opposed him he could do nothing, but if their minds were sympathetic and not antagonistic he would succeed.

The speeches of Mr. Fletcher and of Yoga Rama still further raised the expectations of the audience that they were about to witness that afternoon a demonstration of the power of mind over mind by supernormal means.

Yoga Rama, after the conclusion of his speech, called for thirty persons (ladies and gentlemen) to come upon the stage and form a Committee. A gentleman and I first answered the call. We were soon followed by a rush of ladies and gentlemen who rather inconveniently filled the stage, but this did not interfere with the performance, as the majority of the ladies and gentlemen kept at the back of the stage while Yoga Rama carried out his experiments with a limited number of the members of the Committee. In order to be more at his ease, Yoga Rama removed his turban. I placed it under a table which stood on the stage. I then had a good look at him. I found he was a black man with short crisp curly hair. From his appearance and the fluency with which he speaks English, I came to the conclusion that he is not an Abyssinian, but an American or West Indian negro.

Amongst the members of the Committee were Mr. Zancig and Mr. William Marriott. Both of these gentlemen I have had the pleasure of knowing for some years. They, together with Mr. Charles Guttwoch (a friend of Mr. Marriott), three or four other gentlemen, and myself, were the only members of the Committee who actively endeavoured to ascertain whether Yoga Rama's experiments depended for their success on trickery or on other causes. The other members of the Committee remained passive spectators. As regards the lady members with whom Yoga Rama tried a few experiments, they declared themselves, at the conclusion of the performance, to be believers in his alleged supernormal claims.

Before the experiments commenced, Yoga Rama asked that some one should blindfold him with some articles which lay on a small table in the centre of the stage. These consisted of two pieces of folded paper just large enough to cover the eyebrows and eyes, a piece of porous plaster perforated with holes, a thin white cotton handkerchief, two gloves, and a long red silk scarf. Mr. Marriott offered to blindfold him. I stood close to him while this was being done. Mr. Marriott placed the pieces of paper first on Yoga Rama's eyes, then the porous plaster, then the cotton handkerchief, after this the two gloves, and finally the red scarf which he wound several times round his head. The tip of Yoga Rama's nose could be seen under the plaster, the white cotton handkerchief, and the scarf. Yoga Rama, who remained standing, then requested some one to sit on a chair in front of him, to think of a name, then to hold his left hand (*i.e.* the sitter's left hand) in front of the sitter's face, and to trace on the palm of the left hand with the forefinger of the right the first letter of the name thought of. The sitter was then asked to give taps on his left hand or make movements in the air with his right hand corresponding to the number of letters of which the name thought of consisted. When Yoga Rama suggested (as he subsequently did) that the name of a flower or of a city should be thought of, he requested that the same procedure of tracing the first letter of the name and giving a number of taps or making movements with the right hand corresponding to the number of letters should be followed, but when he suggested that a play of Shakespeare should be thought of he only asked that the first one or two letters of the title should be traced on the palm of the left hand of the sitter with the forefinger of the other hand. He did not then ask that taps or movements of the right hand should be given or made. About an hour and a half of the first part of the performance was taken up by experiments of the above nature. These were varied only by one experiment of telling the title of a hymn which a lady thought of, one of reading the thoughts of a young lady, and one experiment with playing cards.

Yoga Rama then made a long speech about happiness depending on our own selves and our being what we willed ourselves to be. He asserted that he had overcome in himself the passion of anger. He laboured these points so much and repeated himself so often that it became manifest he was making the speech solely with the object of filling up the time.

The patience of the Acting Committee became exhausted, and one of the members advanced to the front of the stage, interrupted Yoga Rama, and, appealing to the audience, said he had no doubt but that he had their support when he asserted that they had come to the theatre not to hear speeches but to witness experiments. Yoga Rama brought his speech abruptly to a close after saying he would now demonstrate the power he had acquired of controlling the functions of his body and of rendering it insensible to pain. To show the control over his body he asked two members of the Committee to stand by his side and to look at their watches and note the length of time he was able to cease from breathing. To show his insensibility to pain he said he would stand barefooted on a board studded with long nails, and also stand on broken glass.

I have given an account of the nature of the performance with which Yoga Rama favoured us. I will now proceed to describe the experiments more in detail and to comment upon them.

Mr. Marriott was the first person to sit on the chair in front of Yoga Rama. He was told to hold his left hand in front of his face, to trace the first letter of the name thought of on the palm of his left hand with the forefinger of the right, and give the taps or make the movements in the air with his right hand in the manner already described. Mr. Marriott, instead of holding his left hand up, held his right hand. Yoga Rama immediately said, "Not your right hand but your left." This was a suspicious circumstance, as it indicated that Yoga Rama could see notwithstanding he was blindfolded. Now conjurers know that blindfolding in the manner above described is not a precaution against seeing, as at the time of blindfolding what the conjurer does is to shut his eyes tightly and bring his eyebrows well down. When the blindfolding is finished, the conjurer opens his eyes and draws his eyebrows up; the bandages will then be displaced and drawn up from their original position and he will be able to see under the bandages through the spaces between the bridge of his nose and his cheeks. This, in the joint opinion of Mr. Zancig, Mr. Marriott, and myself, is what Yoga Rama did, and our opinion was confirmed when we examined the bandages at the time they were removed from the performer's eyes, as will be described later.

Yoga Rama's method of telling the name thought of is to watch the movement of the finger of the sitter's right hand while he traces the first letter of the name on the palm of the left. This indicates to him the first letter of the name, then he counts the number of taps or movements given by the sitter's right hand. Thus, if the first letter were W and the number of taps or movements seven, the name in all likelihood would be William, or, if the first letter were W and the number of taps or movements six, the name would probably be Walter. Ordinary Christian names are limited in number, and Yoga Rama took care to know beforehand whether the sitter were thinking of a female name or of a male name. It was therefore not a difficult matter for him to hit upon the name. Moreover, when he was in doubt, as was often the case, he not only asked that the first letter should be traced, but the second and the third and the fourth, etc. Before hazarding a guess Yoga Rama often asked whether the second or third or fourth, etc., letter of the name were a letter that he mentioned. Thus, if he were not quite sure that W had been traced, but he had noticed that seven taps or movements had been given, he would say is not the fourth letter of the name L. If the sitter answered in the affirmative, he would be pretty sure that William was the name, but if the sitter's answer were a negative one, Yoga Rama asked that the letters should be traced again and the taps, etc., repeated. Yoga Rama resorted to the above-described method when he asked the sitter to think of the name of a flower or of a city, but he only tried one or two experiments with the names of flowers or cities, the reason being, obviously, that as the names of flowers or cities are not so limited in number as Christian names, he fought shy of them. The reason he gave for not being able to guess readily the name of a flower was, he said, that he was not a botanist.

As regards the titles of Shakespeare's plays he only asked that one or two of the first letters of the title should be traced on the left hand, and did not require any taps or movements of the right hand. Any person acquainted with Shakespeare's plays and knowing the first one or two letters of the title could have guessed with equal facility which play was in the mind of the sitter. After getting the name of the play, Yoga Rama asked the sitter to think of a personage in that play. He only requested that this should be done once or twice, and was not successful in getting the name of the personage at the first guess, but only after making two or three guesses.

In the experiment of telling the title of a hymn which a lady had in her mind, Yoga Rama resorted to the same method of asking her to trace the first letter of the title of the hymn on the palm of her left hand. She traced the letter L, and he hazarded the guess that it was "Lead, kindly light," which proved to be correct. Apparently the most successful experiments were one carried out with a young lady and one with myself. Yoga Rama asked the young lady to think of something. He then, without asking her to trace any letter or make movements with her right hand, told her that she wished to get married. She acknowledged that that was the thought in her mind. This caused a good deal of amusement amongst the audience. The young lady left the stage immediately after the experiment. This step on her part gave rise in the minds of some of the members of the Committee that she was an accomplice, and that, as the experiment had been carried out, she was no longer required by Yoga Rama. These members of the Committee may be doing an injustice to the young lady, but it was unfortunate she should have left the stage at that moment.

As regards the experiment with myself, I stood in front of Yoga Rama and did not sit down, neither did I place my left hand in front of my face as other experimenters had done, but close against my body when tracing the letters of my second name, which was the one I had in my mind.

My object in standing up was to have my hands out of the line of his vision. I took care that the movement of the forefinger of my right hand when tracing the letters should not be seen by him.

Yoga Rama repeatedly asked me to trace and retrace all the letters of the name. He then gave the name correctly. Although this experiment appeared to indicate that the performer possessed telepathic powers, it must be borne in mind that he might have known who I was, as he had been practising his so-called occult powers for some time in London under the name of Professor Pickens before he assumed that of Yoga Rama. It was not necessary that he should see my face in order to know with whom he was experimenting. It was observed that he took a very careful stock of the dresses of the Acting Committee before he was blindfolded. It was only necessary, therefore, that he should see the lower part of the dress for him to know which member of the Committee stood in front of him. As one member after the other experimented with him he described their dress. He asserted that he was able to do this by a sort of telepathic vision.

The experiment with the playing cards was a simple conjuring trick. Yoga Rama produced a pack of cards and asked the Committee to see that it was unopened. I opened the pack, shuffled the cards, and handed them to Mr. Marriott, who had been asked by the Professor to retire to a corner of the stage and choose a card which he was to show to two members of the Committee. Mr. Guttwoch and I accompanied Mr. Marriott to the corner of the stage and saw which card Mr. Marriott had chosen. Mr. Marriott then shuffled the pack again and handed it to Yoga Rama, who put it in his pocket. Yoga Rama then asked Mr. Marriott what card he had chosen. Mr. Marriott informed him. He then wrote something on a piece of paper which he folded and handed to one of the members of the Committee to hold. He then drew from his pocket another pack of cards similar in appearance to the original pack (that it was not the original pack was evidenced by the fact that the bottom card of the pack which Yoga Rama drew from his pocket was not the same as the bottom card of the original pack), but which had the cards arranged in an order known to Yoga Rama. He proceeded to pass the cards one after the other before Mr. Marriott's eyes, asking him to tell him when he came to the card he had chosen. When Yoga Rama came to the card, Mr. Marriott told him. Yoga Rama then said, "What is the card in front of the one you chose and the one behind it?" He was informed which they were. He then asked that the piece of paper should be opened, and it was found that the names of the cards had been written by him on the piece of paper. What occult power Yoga Rama intended to demonstrate by this simple conjuring trick I fail to see. It could not have been telepathy, as the two cards (the names of which Yoga Rama had written) had not been chosen nor thought of by Mr. Marriott.

A few words will suffice to describe the experiments which Yoga Rama carried out to show (1) the control he had acquired over the functions of his body, and (2) his insensibility to pain. As has already been stated, he asked two members of the Committee to stand by him and note by their watches the length of time that he was able to cease breathing. He retained his breath for fifty seconds. A member of the Committee at the back of the stage called out, when the length of time was announced, "That is nothing. I can stop breathing for a full minute." This exclamation appeared to disconcert Yoga Rama a good deal. The standing barefooted on a board studded with nails and on broken glass are common tricks which can be seen performed by negroes at country fairs. I felt the points of the nails and found they had been filed down and were blunt. Mr. Marriott sat on the nails to the amusement of the audience while Yoga Rama had gone off the stage to remove his boots. When Yoga Rama returned he stood barefooted on these nails only for about half a minute. He then proceeded to break some bottles on a piece of felt. He pounded away on the glass with a hammer till he had reduced the greater part to nearly a powder. He carefully pushed the larger pieces of glass on one side and stood on the powdered portion.

I will now proceed to state the reasons which lead me to the conclusion that Yoga Rama was able to see, although apparently blindfolded.

1. The bandages were removed from his eyes by Mr. Marriott, who had blindfolded him at the commencement of the performance. While this was being done I had my face about two feet away from Yoga Rama's face and I carefully noted the position of each article as it was being removed. The lower edge of the porous plaster was above the tip of the performer's nose, and the edge of the white handkerchief above the edge of the plaster, and above the edge of the handkerchief was the edge of the crimson scarf. The edges of the handkerchief and scarf were sufficiently high up, so that, had the blindfolding depended only on these, he could have seen under them. The gloves which had been placed on the handkerchief need not be taken into account, as the folded pieces of paper on his eyes prevented them from pressing into the sockets of Yoga Rama's eyes, and he, by merely closing the eyes and bringing the eyebrows well down when he was being blindfolded and then opening his eyes and lifting the eyebrows well up, could displace the gloves from their original position and cause them to rise, as a conjurer well knows; therefore the blindfolding really depended on the position of the porous plaster. Now when Mr. Marriott placed the plaster over the pieces of paper he took care that the lower edges of both pieces should be on one of the lines of holes which existed in the plaster as shown in the accompanying engraving (which is taken from a photograph).

He also took care that the lower edge of the plaster should stick against Yoga Rama's cheeks. On examining the plaster just before it was removed we found that the lower edge no longer stuck against the performer's cheeks. There were hollow spaces between the bridge of his nose and his cheeks through which he could have seen with a downward glance. The point now arises whether he used both his eyes or only one. I noticed that Yoga Rama always kept the right side of his face towards the sitters when trying the experiments. If the reader will look at the engraving, which shows the exact position of the folded pieces of paper at the time of the removal of the plaster from Yoga Rama's face, he will see that the piece of paper which covered his right eye is no longer on the same line of holes as the left piece, but is higher up, and, what is most suspicious, he will note some pieces of tissue paper which were stuck on the plaster by Yoga Rama and were under the pieces of folded paper, which prevented these from adhering to the plaster; thus by an upper movement of the eyebrows Yoga Rama succeeded in raising the folded piece of paper which covered his right eye, and with this eye he glanced under the plaster and watched the movements of the sitter's hands, etc.

2. As I have stated above, Yoga Rama always kept the right side of his head towards the person with whom he was experimenting. He tried one experiment with a gentleman who sat in the second row of the stalls. He then turned his body round so that the right side of his face was in the same position relatively to this gentleman as it had been to the sitters on the stage. Moreover, the lights in the body of the theatre were not alight when Yoga Rama was trying his alleged thought-readings with the members of the Committee on the stage, but when he experimented with the gentleman in the stalls, one of the electric chandeliers in the body of the theatre, not far from the gentleman, was immediately lit, thus enabling Yoga Rama to watch the movements of the gentleman's right hand when tracing the letters of the name he had chosen on the palm of his left hand, and giving the taps corresponding to the number of the letters.

3. At the conclusion of the performance, after the bulk of the audience had left, some persons remained in the foyer of the theatre, and a discussion arose, during which some of the persons present asserted that Yoga Rama had brought about his results by supernormal means. Mr. Marriott, Mr. Guttwoch, and I denied this. At that moment Yoga Rama came into the foyer, and he was accused by us of having been able to see. He asserted that he had not seen, and to prove it offered to try some experiments while a handkerchief was held tightly against his eyes. Mr. Guttwoch held a handkerchief against his eyes. As Yoga Rama was not now able to see, he resorted to a different method from the one he used on the stage. He held the wrist of the left hand of a lady with the thumb and three fingers of his right hand, while his forefinger rested against the back of the lady's hand. He then asked her to trace the letters of the name thought of with the forefinger of her right hand on the palm of her left hand, which was being

held by him. He was able to tell the name, but only after repeated tracing of the letters by the lady. Yoga Rama not being able to be guided by sight as in his stage performances, now guided himself by the sense of touch. Although I have never before carried out an experiment of this nature myself, when Miss Newton and I returned to the rooms of the Society for Psychical Research I tried the experiment with her. I closed my eyes and held her wrist, and was able to feel the letter which she traced on the palm of her hand. Manifestly this is a difficult trick to perform, and requires great practice. I noticed that Yoga Rama chose the hand of a lady in preference to that of a gentleman, obviously because a lady's hand is thinner than that of a man, and the motion of her finger would be more easily felt.

What convinced me more than any of the above reasons that Yoga Rama was able to see during his performance is the following fact. I placed the sticking plaster over my eyes after it had been taken from Yoga Rama's eyes and, to my surprise, I found I could perfectly well see through it. The numerous small holes with which it was perforated allowed me to do this.

The audience at the "Little Theatre" had had their expectations raised that they were to witness manifestations of the occult powers of the mind through the mediumship of an Abyssinian Yogi, instead of which they witnessed an ordinary conjuring entertainment by a man who previously to assuming the name of "Yoga [sic] Rama" was known as Professor A. D. Pickens of Conduit Street, London.

Besides the method used by Yoga Rama for producing his so-called thought transference, there are others resorted to by public entertainers. The one most in use is by means of a verbal code. The letters of the alphabet are substituted and a word can be conveyed by the agent asking a series of questions, each question beginning with a substituted letter. The percipient has to remember what letters the substituted ones represent; he takes note of the first letter only of each question, puts them together in his mind, and thus gets the word that it is the intention of the agent to convey.

I have made a table (shown opposite) which shows one of these systems.

If the name "Alfred" is to be conveyed, it can be done by the following questions:—

Here is a name	= A
Can you see it?	= L
Endeavour to do so	= F
Mind what you are doing	= R
Go on	= D

The letter E is understood.

TABLE

SUBSTITUTED LETTERS TABLE			NUMBERS TABLE
A is H	J is L	S is N	No. 1 is Say
B " T	K " Pray	T " P	" 2 " Be
C " S	L " C	V " Look	" 3 " Can
D " G	M " O	W " R	" 4 " Do
E " F	N " D	X " See this	" 5 " Will
F " E	O " V	Y " Q	" 6 " What
G " A	P " J	Z " Hurry	" 7 " Please
H " I	Q " W		" 8 " Are
I " B	R " M		" 9 " Now
			" 10 " Tell

SETS			
SET A	SET B	SET C	SET D
What is this?	*What article is this?*	*What is it made of?*	*What colour?*
No. 1. Watch	No. 1. Handkerchief	No. 1. Gold	No. 1. White
" 2. Bracelet	" 2. Necktie	" 2. Silver	" 2. Black
" 3. Guard	" 3. Bag	" 3. Copper	" 3. Blue

" 4. Chain	" 4. Glove	" 4. Lead	" 4. Brown
" 5. Breastpin	" 5. Purse	" 5. Zinc	" 5. Red
" 6. Necklace	" 6. Basket	" 6. Wood	" 6. Green
" 7. Ring	" 7. Book	" 7. Brass	" 7. Yellow
" 8. Rosary	" 8. Head-dress	" 8. Paper	" 8. Grey
" 9. Cross	" 9. Fan	" 9. Silk	" 9. Purple
" 10. Charm	" 10. Key	" 10. Glass	" 10. Violet

The transmission of the nature of an article is by dividing articles that would be likely to be brought to a public entertainment into sets of ten, each set being indicated by a different question. These sets have to be learned by heart by the agent and the percipient. I give in the table four sets to illustrate my meaning. After asking the question which conveys the set to which the article belongs, a second question is asked, beginning with the word corresponding to the number on the number table. This will indicate what number in the set the article corresponds to. As an example: when the question "What is this?" is asked, it means that the article corresponds to Set A. If the second question begins with "Do," such as "Do you know?", this question on referring to the number table would mean No. 4; therefore the article would be a chain. Now, if the question "What is it made of?" is asked, it would refer to Set C, and if this question is followed by "Can you tell me?", on referring to the number table it will be found to correspond to No. 3; therefore the article would be a chain made of copper. When an article is not in any one of the sets the substituted letter code is used. Of course public entertainers learn by heart a number of sets, not only four.

For silent thought transference occasionally electrical contrivances are resorted to. These are placed in different parts of the hall, and when being pressed by the foot or hand of the agent will convey a message to a certain part of the stage upon which the percipient (who may be blindfolded) rests his foot.

There is another silent method which can be worked by a confederate who is placed behind a curtain close to the chair on the stage upon which the blindfolded percipient sits. The confederate watches the performer who stands amongst the audience and reads through a spyglass what he is writing on his tablet when putting down what members of the audience wish to be done. The confederate then communicates the contents of the writing to the percipient on the stage by whispering or by an electrical apparatus. The position of the performer or agent while he is writing in a clear hand on his tablets with his back to the stage easily enables a confederate to read the writing.

Then there is the silent method of a French conjurer, some of whose performances I have witnessed, which consists of suggesting or "forcing" the spectators to do certain things, each action having a corresponding number which he conveys to his lady assistant, who is blindfolded, by touching her foot with his after she has come down from the stage and stands by his side amongst the audience.

The "time-coding" method consists of silently counting by the agent and percipient at the same rate, starting from a preconcerted signal and ending at another preconcerted signal. The performer amongst the audience has in his hand a piece of paper on which is written the number that he wishes to silently convey to the other blindfolded performer on the stage. At the moment that he bends his head to look at the number he begins silently counting at a certain rate; a confederate behind the scenes begins counting at the same rate from the moment that the performer bends his head. When the performer lifts his head he ceases counting, so does the confederate. Each number written on the paper is thus conveyed, and the confederate communicates the total to the blindfolded performer by means of an electrical apparatus or otherwise.

I have attended several performances in public halls in London at which thought transference—so-called—was carried out by the above trick methods.

Sir Oliver Lodge was present with me at one of the performances at which the time-coding method was used. He has sent me the following note:—

"I was with Mr. Baggally on one of these occasions, and took note of the fact that he could often guess what was being transmitted by the performers quite as well as they could themselves. We sat in a box looking at them, and he often told me before they had spoken what they were going to say (or words to that effect).

"I perceived even without his assistance that the performance, which was stimulated by the success of the Zancigs, was an exceedingly inferior imitation of what they had achieved, and was manifestly done by a code of some kind.

"O. J. L."

Some of the methods resorted to by public entertainers are so ingenious that the spectator is led to believe that genuine thought transference has taken place. The following correspondence, which appeared in the spiritualistic weekly paper called *Light,* illustrates a case in point. In the number of *Light* of the 25th October 1902 there appeared this letter headed "Thought Transference":—

"SIR,—A few years ago Mr. and Mrs. Baldwin gave the following entertainment in almost every large town in the three kingdoms. The public were invited to write any question or questions they desired to have answered on a piece of paper, to place it in their pockets, and keep it there without communicating its contents to anyone, and then when they went to the hall their names were called out and their question answered without the papers leaving their possession. About fifty such inquiries were answered each evening without a single failure by Mrs. Baldwin, who sat blindfolded with her back to the audience. From my experience and that of my friends, collusion was impossible, and the only way of accounting for the performance was by thought transference or telepathy between Mrs. Baldwin and those of the audience with whom she was in mental sympathy.

(Signed)   "C. A. M."

Commenting on this letter, I wrote to *Light*, and my communication appeared the following week. It was to this effect:—

"Under the heading of 'Thought Transference,' your correspondent, C. A. M., gives an account of some entertainments by Mr. and Mrs. Baldwin, at which he says" (I here quoted from C. A. M.'s letter, and then continued as follows):—"I never was present at entertainments given by Mr. and Mrs. Baldwin, and therefore cannot express an opinion as to the *modus operandi* in their particular case, but I would point out that their entertainments bear a close resemblance to those given by conjurers. The explanation of the mystery in a conjurer's case is as follows:—The conjurer asks members of the audience to write their questions secretly, to sign their names at the bottom of the question, and then to fold the pieces of paper on which the questions are written and place them in their pockets. To facilitate the writing he hands pencils round and tablets upon which to rest the pieces of paper during the writing of the questions, or the members of the audience, if they so wish, can retire into an adjoining room and write their questions on a table. The tablets and pencils are then collected by an assistant who is a confederate, who then retires from the hall to the room where the table is. The tablets and table have false surfaces of leather or other material, which, on being removed by the confederate, disclose a layer of carbon paper resting on another of white paper upon which the questions have been recorded unknown to the inquirers. The confederate then proceeds to read the questions with their respective attached signatures, and to communicate them to the blindfolded medium by an electrical apparatus upon which the medium's foot rests, or by other mechanical means."

I signed my letter W. W. B. A fortnight after, the following letter appeared in *Light*:—

"Sir,—With reference to the communication by W. W. B. referring to the supposed thought transference, and mentioned by another correspondent, C. A. M., in connection with the entertainments of Professor Baldwin (an American conjurer and brother mason), whom I met in Cape Town on two separate occasions, permit me to state that (1) if it is the same Baldwin, he is one of the cleverest illusionists in his special line of trick thought transference, and W. W. B. is quite right. (2) I know that Mr. and Mrs. Baldwin did most of their experiments by trick, because, being one of the chosen committee to test the so-called thought reading, I fixed it absolutely as trickery on the lines indicated by W. W. B.

(Signed)   "BERKS HUTCHINSON"

I was gratified to read this letter and to find that my conjecture was correct that the Baldwin performance was a mere exhibition of conjuring.

PART III

THE ZANCIGS

Some years ago there appeared at the Alhambra Theatre, London, two entertainers—Mr. and Mrs. Zancig—whose performances were of so puzzling a nature that to many who had witnessed them the only explanation of the results obtained appeared to be that genuine telepathy was at play. The *Daily Mail* newspaper arranged that Mr. and Mrs. Zancig should be subjected to a series of severe tests at its office, and on the 30th November 1906 these were carried out.

On the 1st December the *Daily Mail* published a full account of these experiments. The publication of this and of other accounts by persons who had witnessed the remarkable performances of the Zancigs led to a heated controversy between the correspondents of the *Daily Mail* and the *Daily Chronicle*. Those of the first paper mostly asserted that the performance was an exhibition of true telepathy, while those of the second paper declared that codes—visual and verbal—would account for the phenomena. Previously to the experiment carried out by the *Daily Mail* I had obtained a letter of introduction to the Zancigs from a friend of mine who had had private tests with them, but as it was necessary to have the permission of the manager of the Alhambra before an interview with the Zancigs could be arranged, I called at the offices of that theatre, and saw Mr. Scott, the manager. I informed him that I was a member of the Society for Psychical Research, which body I told him took the deepest interest in telepathy. I handed him a letter that I had written to Mr. Zancig, and on the 29th November 1906 I received the following communication from the last-named gentleman:—

"DEAR SIR,—I received a letter from Miss H. A. Dallas, telling me that you would like to meet us. Now, my dear sir, we would be pleased to make your acquaintance, and have you call for a visit, but if it is for any private show and to be tried and judged if our work is, as we represent, 'two minds with but a single thought,' I will have to say No. We have done nothing since we arrived in London but have callers to test and try us every day, from three to four ladies and gentlemen. My wife and I agreed to all tests they put to us, and all was quite satisfactory. Personally I do not care, but it has been quite a strain on my wife. Should you care to witness our show, you would be able to see us at ten p.m. on the Alhambra stage, but if you care to call and see us, and have a little talk, we both would be pleased to meet you.— Trusting that I am understood, I remain, yours sincerely,

(Signed)   "JULIUS ZANCIG"

Although the contents of the above letter were of a discouraging nature, I determined to strike the iron while it was hot; therefore, on the evening of the same day I called, accompanied by my wife, at the flat where the Zancigs resided. They were at the time partaking of their evening meal. We apologized for our intrusion, but by the kind way that they received us we were soon put at our ease. I informed Mr. Zancig that I was much interested in telepathy, and that I had personally carried out experiments in this branch of psychical research, and that I was assured of the truth of its existence through the successes that I had obtained.

Mr. and Mrs. Zancig impressed my wife and myself most favourably by their unaffected and simple manner. After a conversation which lasted about ten minutes, Mr. Zancig very kindly spontaneously offered to try some experiments. I will now describe these. Madame Zancig went to the other end of the room farthest away from where Mr. Zancig, my wife, and I sat. She faced the wall with her back to us; Mr. Zancig then wrote with a chalk a line of figures on a slate which he held in his left hand, and called out the word "Ready." Madame Zancig immediately named the figures correctly and in their proper order. The same kind of experiment was tried successfully three times. The results might have been due to telepathy, but I was not satisfied, as it could have been possible that the figures were prearranged, or that Madame Zancig could tell by the sound of the chalk what figures were being written. I also had in my mind the fact that there is a method of communicating figures by time-coding.

Mr. Zancig then asked me to write a double line of figures. I handed the slate to him, and after he had called out "Ready" Madame Zancig proceeded to cast them up correctly.

As Madame Zancig named all my figures aloud as she was summing them up, this experiment was of a more complicated nature than the previous ones; nevertheless, I was not entirely satisfied, as time-coding in putting down the resultant figures by Mr. Zancig, and the hearing of the sound of the chalk by Madame Zancig when I was writing my own figures, might have accounted for the favourable result.

To prevent the possibility of communicating by an electrical or other apparatus concealed under the carpet, I requested Mr. Zancig to raise his feet from the floor. He immediately complied by sitting on the table, where he remained to the last experiment.

Madame Zancig then retired into an adjoining bedroom with a slate in her hand; the door was closed, but not entirely. My wife wrote down two lines of figures, the slate was handed by her to Mr. Zancig, who called out "Ready," and he then proceeded without speaking to add them up. Madame Zancig then came into the room with the correct result written by herself on her slate. This was a more crucial test than the last, but still, although visual-coding was excluded, sound-coding while Mr. Zancig was writing the resultant sum was not entirely so.

Then followed the experiment of transmitting a selected line in a book. Mr. Zancig handed me a book and asked me to open it at any page and to point out a line. After I had done so I handed the book to him. He called out "Ready." Then his wife opened a duplicate book at the proper page, and read the line which I had selected. Doubtless the words of the line were not communicated telepathically or otherwise by Mr. Zancig, but only the number of the page and the number of the line counting from the top of the page. Nevertheless, it was difficult to discover by what method this was done, as Mr. Zancig simply called out "Ready." There did not appear to be time for the numbers of the page and line to be transmitted by time-coding. The reader will observe that as the experiments proceeded they appeared to present increasing evidence that true telepathy was at work.

The following and last experiment that I tried on this occasion was the most crucial. I requested Mr. Zancig to go out with me on to the landing outside the door of the flat. I did not previously inform Madame Zancig nor Mr. Zancig of the nature of the test that I was about to put. Madame Zancig remained in the room with my wife. The door was closed, but not completely. When we were on the landing I suddenly drew my cheque-book out of my pocket, tore out a cheque, and handed it to Mr. Zancig, requesting him to transmit the number. Mr. Zancig observed to me in a whisper that the noise of the traffic in the street was very disturbing. This was true, as the hall door to the street was open. He then remained silent while he looked at the cheque. My wife then came out on to the landing, and handed me a slate upon which Madame Zancig had during the experiment written the words, "In the year 1875." Mr. Zancig then said aloud, "This is not what we want; it is the number." My wife returned into the room with the slate, and the door was closed, but not completely. It was impossible, however, for Madame Zancig to see her husband. The suspicion arose in my mind that the number on the cheque might have been communicated to Madame Zancig by the words that Mr. Zancig had spoken aloud. I therefore took the cheque that he had in his hand and substituted another one with a different number that I tore from the bottom of my cheque-book. Mr. Zancig remained absolutely silent during the whole time that this second experiment lasted. My wife again came out of the room with the slate, upon which Madame Zancig had written quite correctly, in their proper order, four of the five numbers of the second cheque, with the exception of the last figure, which was wanting, but just as we were returning to the room Madame Zancig said, "There was another figure; it was four"—which was correct. This impressed me as a good test, with regard to the three last numbers of this cheque, which were different from the corresponding ones of the first cheque. Madame Zancig could not see her husband, and he remained absolutely silent while the experiment was being carried out.

I insert here a note by Sir Oliver Lodge in which he gives an account of an experiment of a similar nature, and also of other experiments which he tried with the Zancigs.

"Independently of the more thorough investigations of Mr. Baggally, I myself was favoured with a private interview with the Zancigs, who were friendly and considerate and helpful; and I tried the experiment of having Mrs. Zancig outside the room, though with door open, and Mr. Zancig with me and quite silent. I wrote five or six figures on a slate, taking care to make no noise, and Mrs. Zancig failed to get them correctly. Zancig seemed distressed at that, and after a little time groaned out, 'Oh, surely you can do this'; almost immediately after which Mrs. Zancig came into the room with the correct figures written on her slate. It was difficult to see how the sentence had conveyed the figures, but it was instructive to find that utterance of some kind seemed necessary. It was partly this, and partly the manifest difficulty of eliminating all possibilities of code between a pair of performers accustomed to go about together, with years of experience behind them, that prevented me from doing what I probably ought to have done, though circumstances did not render it very easy, namely, to make a serious study of the Zancig phenomena.

"Moreover, I questioned Mr. Zancig about codes, and found that he was familiar with a great many. He was quite frank about it, and rather implied, as I thought, that at times he was ready to use any code or other normal kind of assistance that might be helpful, though he assured me that he found that he and his wife did possess a faculty which they did not in the least understand, but which was more efficient and quicker than anything they could get by codes. On the whole, I think this extremely likely, but the rapidity and the certainty and dependableness of the power went far beyond anything that I could imagine as possible between people who depended on supernormal faculty alone. But if there was a mixture of devices between people so skilled, I despaired of bringing the genuine part of the phenomenon to a definite issue.

"I do not think that either this or the weight of my other avocations are a sufficient excuse for this neglect, but it certainly was not easy to get opportunities for careful investigation. One of the main difficulties was that they were not free agents, having entered into contracts with managers whose financial interests partly depended upon the continued uncertainty of the public as to the causes underlying their very remarkable performance.

Moreover, I knew that so skilled an investigator as Mr. Baggally was more favourably impressed with them than I was myself, and was able to give to them some considerable time and attention.

"The extraordinary and rapid success with which Mrs. Zancig named one thing after another, handled or seen by her husband as he went through the hall in their public performances, is familiar to everybody who attended those exhibitions; but one episode which I have not put on record did impress me as rather exceptionally good, though entirely unsensational and unnoticeable at the time. I relate it here:—

"The Zancigs happened to come to Birmingham for a week during the University Vacation when I was away. On the last day of their performance I happened unexpectedly to return to Birmingham, and was dining at the club with some other men. Some one remarked that the Zancigs were performing, and suggested that we should cut dessert and go and see them; so we went in the middle of the performance and sat at the back of the gallery. Everything went on as usual. Mrs. Zancig was on the stage, blindfolded, I think, though I attach no importance to that. Mr. Zancig had been through the body of the hall, and was coming along the side gallery, taking objects from members of the audience as he went, and having them described quickly one after the other as usual, when he caught sight of me at the back of the gallery, and indicated recognition by a little start. The next object that he took in hand (a purse or what not) he said, 'What is this?' and Madame Zancig on the stage said 'Oliver.' Zancig shook his head and muttered, 'No, that's what I was thinking of, but what's this?' On which she said whatever it was correctly, and the performance went on as usual; my friends in due time getting their tests efficiently done. Nobody noticed the incident in particular; it was over in a second. It conveyed no impression of anything except of a slight confusion,—an error, in fact, immediately corrected,—but I could not fail to notice that the very unimportant incident tended in favour of the view that a power of sympathy or communication between them was genuine, since she got an undesired and unintended impression which certainly was at the moment in Mr. Zancig's mind.

"O. J. L."

Later, on the same evening of the experiment with the numbers on my cheque-book which I have described above, my wife and I attended the public performance at the Alhambra. We were seated at a distance from the stage. When Mr. Zancig came amongst the audience my wife handed him a piece of something black, the nature of which it was difficult to tell at first sight. He stooped down and asked in a whisper, "What is that?" My wife answered, also in a whisper, "Liquorice." Madame Zancig immediately called out from the stage, "Liquorice." No word had been spoken by Mr. Zancig after my wife had whispered the word "Liquorice." I then handed a visiting-card with a double name. Zancig read to himself in a low voice the last name, which was Hutchinson, and said, "What is the first name?" Madame Zancig called out "Berks"; this was correct. It appeared to me suspicious, however, that the question, "What is the first name?" although appropriate and natural, should contain the same number of words as there are letters in the name Berks—namely, five. Therefore some months after, at another performance, I wrote the same name, Berks Hutchinson, on a piece of paper and handed it to Mr. Zancig. This time he asked, "What is this?" Madame Zancig replied, "A piece of paper with a name." Mr. Zancig said, "Give the name." She replied, "Berks Hutchinson."

I attended a series of performances at the Alhambra, and took down the questions and answers in order, if possible, to discover the code. On witnessing a first performance the spectator might be led to believe that word-coding alone is at the bottom of the mystery, but if notes are taken at a number of performances he will find that the same question is answered differently time after time.

From my experiments with the Zancigs I came to the conclusion that although the alleged transmission of thought might possibly depend on a code or codes which I was unable to unravel, yet their performance was of such a nature that it was worthy of serious scientific examination. On the assumption that they possessed genuine telepathic powers it would be a pity that the opportunity of investigating their claim should be missed. I therefore set myself to work to arrange with Mr. Alfred Moul, managing director of the Alhambra, and Mr. Zancig for some experiments to be tried before a Committee of the members of the Society for Psychical Research.

An article appeared in the *Daily Mail*, inspired evidently by Mr. Moul, from which I now quote:—

"We have suggested to Mr. Zancig that in preference to inquiries into telepathy by unskilled persons he should place himself in the hands of the Society for Psychical Research, of which Mr. Gerald Balfour is the President, and of which Sir Oliver Lodge, Sir William Crookes, and other distinguished scientists are leading members. Mr. Zancig has informed us that he has already received a communication from that Society, and that he was entirely willing to place himself and Madame Zancig at the disposal of the Society for a thoroughly scientific series of tests."

The investigation by the Society for Psychical Research, at which I was present, took place on the 18th January 1907. I regret that I cannot give an account of what took place at this meeting, as it was mutually arranged between Mr. Moul and the S.P.R. that the results should not be divulged. They appeared, however, sufficiently favourable to some of the members present (though not to all) to induce them to subsequently form an unofficial Committee to carry out further tests. These unofficial experiments did not take place till 26th July 1907.

In the meantime I continued my own private experiments. A striking one is the following. I was in the balcony of the Alhambra on the 19th January 1907, and when Mr. Zancig came to that part of the house I handed him a piece of paper on which I had written the word "Istapalapan." I took care that he should not see the word previously to my giving him the paper. Zancig remarked to me in a whisper, "This is a long word." Owing to the distance from his wife it could not have been possible for her to overhear these words. Then Mr. Zancig called out, "Spell this." Madame Zancig immediately wrote on the blackboard which was on the stage "Istapala," and when she came to the second "p" she wrote "f" and then "san." I have often noticed that when Madame Zancig makes a mistake in a letter or number there is a similarity in the form of the letter or number to that which was to be transmitted; thus, she would put down "f" for "p," "7" for "9." "fsan" in this case is very like "pan," and Mr. Zancig may have mistaken the letters. I fail to understand how in this experiment he was able to code such a long word as "Istapalafsan" by the simple words "Spell this." It would appear as if Madame Zancig really saw what Mr. Zancig was looking at. The reader will recollect that in his preliminary remarks at each of his performances Zancig says, "What I see, Madame Zancig sees."

I have several times observed this alleged peculiarity, notably so on the occasion of the tests at the Gramophone offices, which took place on the 22nd February 1907, and at which I was one of the members of the Committee. Mr. and Mrs. Zancig were divided by a large screen. They could not see each other. A recording trumpet was placed near each, into which they spoke. A table was placed by the side of Mr. Zancig on which a great number of articles had been placed by the members of the Committee. Madame Zancig with great rapidity named the articles as Mr. Zancig took them up in answer to his "What is this? and this?" etc. An incident which struck me as remarkable was the following. Mr. Zancig raised a pencil, saying, "What is this?" and after Madame Zancig had correctly stated what it was, he took up immediately (not in the vicinity of the pencil, but some distance from it) a case, and said, "And this?" Instead of naming the article Madame Zancig proceeded to enumerate in their proper order the articles that lay between the two articles which Mr. Zancig had taken up. Thus, a pencil, a seal, a penknife, a case. It appeared as if Madame Zancig had actually seen the articles over which her husband had passed his hand.

An excellent test was the following. Dr. W. M'Dougall, a member of the Council of the S.P.R., who was present at these tests, borrowed a book from one of the members of the Committee. He came to the side of the screen where Mr. Zancig stood, opened the book at a certain page, then pointed to the middle of a line in the centre of the page. Mr. Zancig, without taking the book in his hand, glanced at the line, then Dr. M'Dougall shut the book, took it to the other side of the screen, and handed it closed to Madame Zancig. Mr. Zancig remained absolutely silent, placed his hand against his forehead, and appeared to make a strong mental effort. Madame Zancig, after the lapse of a minute, opened the book at the proper page and began reading at the word in the middle of the line that had been chosen by Dr. M'Dougall. Some members of the Committee and I stood quite close to Mr. Zancig. We did not hear him utter a sound. He could not be seen by Madame Zancig owing to the screen.

I was present at the *matinée* performance given under the auspices of the *Daily Mirror* newspaper at the Alhambra. Dr. H., principal surgeon of a well-known hospital, handed to Mr. Zancig a set of skeins of silk of different colours. These were then passed on to Madame Zancig, who was on the stage. Dr. H. pointed silently to a skein of silk of a corresponding set which he had retained, and which he took care Madame Zancig could not see. Mr. Zancig, who preserved absolute silence, and remained motionless, looked at the colour of the skein, and in the space of half a minute his wife picked out a skein of the corresponding colour from the set that she had in her possession. This test was tried successfully three times. I particularly took note that Mr. Zancig remained silent and motionless, retaining the same position of his body during the course of the three experiments.

I have tried tests with Mr. and Madame Zancig in the transmission of diagrams. I took with me to a private house to which I was invited an envelope containing cards with diagrams on them. Madame Zancig sat behind a large screen at the end of the room. By her side sat a lady, a friend of mine, who watched Madame Zancig and saw that she did not move from her chair. Mr. Zancig stood close to me near the other end of the room. I presented the envelope to him, retaining it in my hand. He drew out one of the cards on which was a diagram not known either to him or to me till he looked at it. He fixed his gaze intently on it, remained motionless, and in a whisper said to me, "Please say ready." I called out, "Ready," and his wife then drew a diagram on a piece of paper, at the same time saying, "Something like half a moon."

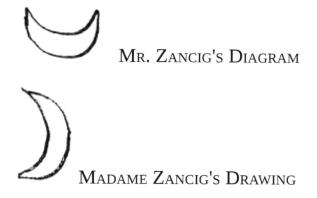

MR. ZANCIG'S DIAGRAM

MADAME ZANCIG'S DRAWING

Mr. Zancig then drew another card from the envelope. This time he did not speak, but nodded his head once, and I called out, "Ready." Madame Zancig thereupon observed, "It is a square within a square." The diagram that Mr. Zancig was looking at was this:

his wife drew this:

Two more cards were then drawn, but Madame Zancig did not succeed; she got absolutely wrong drawings.

At a public performance at Eastbourne I handed Mr. Zancig this diagram:

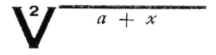

He called out, "Draw this." Madame Zancig, who was on the platform, said, "It is something like this." She made a motion with her right arm like drawing a capital V; she then drew it on the blackboard. After this she slowly drew a horizontal line through the V, thus:

Mr. Zancig said, "Give the number." She then placed a 2 in the proper position. He then called out, "Give the rest." She thereupon placed the *a* under the line, thus:

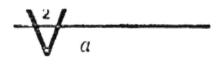

Mr. Zancig said, "What more?" His wife placed the sign of + correctly, but she rubbed it out several times as if in doubt. Finally she put down the sign of + and a capital X, so that her drawing appeared like this:

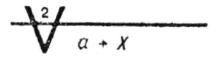

I have had many other experiments with this gifted couple, but have not yet obtained the crucial test of getting Mr. Zancig to be in a distant room with closed doors, while his wife was in another room. The possibility of their using a sound code at one time and a visual code at another is therefore not entirely precluded.

Although I have been quite unable to discover the methods by which they can possibly communicate when a visual and a sound code are not detected, yet I will reserve my ultimate opinion until I obtain tests under the crucial conditions that I have named.

Not only did I personally meet with difficulties in endeavouring to explain the performances of Mr. and Madame Zancig, but also the members of the unofficial Committee that I have referred to. I now give an extract from our unofficial report.

"... It must be remembered that the antecedent probabilities in favour of a code to explain all performances of this kind are enormous.

"While we are of opinion that the records of experiments in telepathy made by the Society for Psychical Research and others raise a presumption for the existence of such a faculty at least strong enough to entitle it to serious scientific attention, the most hopeful results hitherto obtained have not been in any way comparable as regards accuracy and precision with those produced by Mr. and Madame Zancig. Further, there is, so far as we are aware, no case of any public performers (including certain recent examples) where the use of a code or apparatus has not been more or less readily discoverable or clearly to be inferred. In considering, therefore, the claim of Mr. and Madame Zancig to the possession of a genuine telepathic faculty, one is faced by the initial difficulty that such a faculty must be regarded as unique in quality, and Mr. and Madame Zancig themselves as unique in kind, a difficulty on the force of which it is not necessary to insist. On the other hand, the difficulty of suggesting by what method, if not by telepathy, they communicate is considerable. Those who have only witnessed the public theatre performances, clever and perplexing as these are, will not appreciate how hard it is to offer any plausible explanation of their *modus operandi*."

In conclusion, I would wish to point out that the establishment of the fact that telepathy is a scientific truth would have bearings of the greatest importance.

It would show that the transmission of thought could occasionally be effected otherwise than by the ordinary sense channels.

It would change the materialistic conception that thought only acts within the limits of the brain.

It would modify the materialistic scientific view of the relation of mind to matter.

I trust that what I have written will act as an incentive to some of my readers to try experiments in this branch of psychical research.[2] It is not enough that a few individuals by patient inquiry and experiment should have been convinced of the reality of telepathy. What is wanted is that scientific men generally, by the record of an overwhelming number of experiments under the strictest test conditions, should be convinced of its truth. Once let them be so, then public conviction will in due time follow.

Meanwhile I feel bound to state that, in spite of initial improbability, the experiences which I myself have had, as partly narrated in this book, especially those briefly summarized in Part I, have convinced me that the telepathic faculty does exist, and that its detection is a genuine extension of scientific knowledge; though much more will have to be done before the bare fact receives its explanation and is permanently incorporated in a coherent system of Science.

9 781835 915851